FROM
VISION
TO
COMPLETION

A GUIDED JOURNEY
THROUGH HOMEBUILDING'S
KEY DECISIONS

FROM VISION TO COMPLETION

A Guided Journey Through Homebuilding's Key Decisions

David Herzog, MBA, MSF

Published by Game Changer Publishing

Paperback ISBN: 978-1-969372-02-5
Hardcover ISBN: 978-1-969372-03-2
Digital ISBN: 978-1-969372-04-9

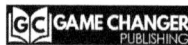

GC | GAME CHANGER PUBLISHING

www.GameChangerPublishing.com

To my mother, **Rita D. Herzog, MSN** —

whose unconditional love has been my foundation, whose guiding light has illuminated my path, and whose steadfast example has convinced me that dreams come true when you keep at them with patience and perseverance. Through every challenge and triumph, you taught me the profound truth that success is not just in achievement, but in the grace with which we pursue it—never forgetting the power and importance of remembering to "be kind first."

ACKNOWLEDGMENTS

I extend my deepest gratitude to my rock and beautiful wife, **Heidi Herzog**; my sister and pillar, **Karen Habighurst**, and **Mark**; my always supportive father, **David Sr.**, and **Debby**; my in-laws—**Bruce**, **Suzanne (aka G-ma)**, **Brad & Katie**, my nephews—**Matt, Drew, Jacob, Ethan, Brennen and Cannon**; my nieces—**Rachel, Katie**, and **Olivia**; and our beloved cats, **Chloe, Charlie, Gracie**, and **Zoey**.

To our champions—**Rich Harrington & family, Al Procopio & family, Ken and Haila Cleaver, Alan and Sara Caldwell, Jeff and Lianne Caruso**, and **Nick and Jenn Keating**.

And finally, to **Robby Bishop, MBA**—my best friend—whose unwavering presence has been with me through every step of this journey.

Read This First

Just to say thanks for buying and reading my book,
I would like to connect with you!

Scan the QR Code or click the link:

https://qrkit.co/ZGaFQ1

FROM
VISION
TO
A GUIDED JOURNEY
THROUGH HOMEBUILDING'S
KEY DECISIONS
COMPLETION

DAVID HERZOG
MBA, MSF

TABLE OF CONTENTS

INTRODUCTION

MY NAME IS DAVID HERZOG, and I'm the founder of Herzog Homes. I consider myself incredibly fortunate to do what I love every day. But more than that, I'm deeply blessed—because none of this has been possible on my own.

From the unconditional love and support of my mother, to the many individuals who have influenced my path—family, friends, mentors, and even those whose challenges taught me valuable lessons— Herzog Homes is built on the foundation of these relationships.

Today, our team has the privilege of doing what we love most: creating exceptional homes and building raving fans along the way.

At my core, I'm a builder—not just of homes, but of relationships, trust, and experiences. Construction is in my blood. I still remember riding my bike past a construction site at age fifteen. Something told me to turn around and ask for a summer job. I did—and Dave Phipps of Phipps Carpentry said yes. That lucky break led to a lifelong career filled with challenges, joy, and pride. From those first days of carrying lumber, sweeping job sites, and dreaming big with

Robby Bishop and Jeff Caruso, we have since delivered more than 2,000 homes and residential lots, developed master-planned communities, and conducted business across Maryland, Virginia, Delaware, Texas, Florida, and now California.

Over the years, we often say, "We've seen it all," and then something new surprises us. However, one thing remains constant: every customer relationship is unique. It fascinates me how different each home-building experience can be, even though the process is largely the same. That's why our focus has always been on the customer experience.

We've spent decades refining that experience, and at its heart, the key is communication—simply knowing what comes next. A third-time homebuyer typically enjoys the process far more than a first-time one because they've learned not to brace for problems but to embrace the journey. We want all our customers to feel that way, whether it's their first build or their third.

So, I wanted to walk you through the process in a relaxed, conversational way—like we're sitting together at a coffee shop. This book isn't meant to dive into complex details or overwhelm you with heavy math. Instead, it offers a clear, step-by-step overview so you always know what's coming next, so you may set your expectations in a way that promotes the best possible experience. The specifics of your journey—such as timelines, paperwork, and local requirements—will ultimately depend on your agent, lender, neighborhood, and city. With that in mind, our team thought it would be helpful to "pull back the curtain" and provide this guidebook, a roadmap, so you aren't navigating blindly.

As you read the pages that follow, I hope you take away two things:

1. Choose your relationships wisely—don't let the lowest price dictate your direction.

2. Enjoy this, truly. Few people get the chance to build a home. You do. Savor the process, celebrate the milestones, and take pride in what you're creating.

Yes, challenges will always arise, but they're manageable. And believe it or not, even the tough moments can bring a little joy.

Welcome to the journey, and let's build something extraordinary together.

David Herzog
Herzog Homes, Founder & CEO

CHAPTER 1

THE WHO, WHAT, AND WHERE OF BUILDING YOUR DREAM HOME

EVERY GREAT JOURNEY begins with a conversation.

Often, it is not in an office, a bank, or even with a builder. It starts around a kitchen table. Maybe it happens during a quiet evening after dinner, or as a spontaneous conversation on the couch, or maybe it's a growing whisper in the back of your mind as you scroll through real estate listings for the tenth night in a row.

What if we built something new?

It is a question filled with excitement and uncertainty, and it marks the start of a remarkable journey.

Building a home is not just a financial transaction. It is a life event. It reflects your hopes, needs, goals, and personal vision. Whether it is your first time or your fifth, the process always begins with that same simple step: the dream.

But turning that dream into something real is where the work begins, and where the real rewards are found.

The Power and Purpose of the Dream

Dreams are powerful because they clarify what matters most. As Disney's *Cinderella* famously sang: *A dream is a wish that your heart makes.*

For some, building a home is driven by necessity. Perhaps your family is expanding, and you need more space. Maybe a job relocation is on the horizon, or you have realized that existing homes in the market simply do not meet your needs.

For others, it is about ambition. You have saved, planned, and now it is time to create a space that is uniquely yours—custom, thoughtful, and built with purpose.

Whatever your motivation, the dream matters. It gives this process meaning and direction. But to move forward, that dream must be translated into specifics, and many people feel overwhelmed by this process.

Let's face it. Homebuilding can feel abstract. It involves plans, permits, inspections, land preparation, and construction loans. It is a world filled with unfamiliar terminology and high-stakes decisions. Without guidance, it is easy to feel lost before you even begin.

But here is the truth. You do not need to know everything right now. What you need is a roadmap and a willingness to learn as you go.

This chapter is the beginning of that roadmap. It introduces the most fundamental questions you must answer before you build. I call them "The Big Three":

1. How much can you afford?
2. Where do you want to build?
3. What type of home fits your needs and lifestyle?

These questions may seem simple, but they will shape every decision you make from this point forward.

The Big Three questions are not independent. They are deeply connected. Your budget will influence where you can build, and where you build will determine what kind of home is realistic.

1. How Much Can You Afford?

Before you explore neighborhoods or floor plans, you need a clear understanding of your financial picture. This is not just about what you want to spend, but about what you can spend wisely and sustainably. This includes your down payment capability (how much you can put down upfront without creating financial stress), your monthly affordability (what you're comfortable paying each month, including taxes, insurance, and utilities), and your loan qualification (what lenders will approve based on your income, credit score, and debt-to-income ratio).

These questions will be explored further in the next chapter. For now, understand that your budget sets the boundaries for everything else.

2. Where Can You Build?

With a financial range in mind, the next question is about location. This is often where dreams meet reality. You may love the idea of building in a popular area, only to discover the land prices are beyond your range, or you may find a hidden gem of a neighborhood that offers more than you expected. Ask yourself what school districts, commute times, and amenities matter to you; whether you prefer suburban developments, rural acreage, or something in between; what infrastructure is available (utilities, roads, internet); and whether the lot is suitable for the type of home you want to build.

Location affects more than cost. It affects quality of life, long-term value, and daily experience.

3. What Can You Build?

Once you have defined your budget and preferred location, you can begin thinking about the design and layout. Consider how many bedrooms and bathrooms you need, whether you prefer an open floor plan, whether you'll need a guest suite, home office, or space for aging parents, and whether energy efficiency, technology integration, or sustainable materials are important to you.

This is where your vision becomes tangible. But remember, what you build must align with where you are building. Lot size, neighborhood covenants, and city codes may influence your options.

It is easy to feel overwhelmed by what you do not know, but starting with what you do know is far more productive. Have you lived in a certain area and liked it? Do you have a preferred layout or square footage in mind? Has someone you know had a good experience with a builder or realtor? These are valuable starting points. Take time to reflect on them, write them down, and discuss them with anyone involved in the decision. Use what you already know to guide your next steps.

You are not alone in this process. People around you can provide critical insight. Friends, coworkers, and family members can help you make better decisions just by sharing their own experiences. Ask questions like who they used for their builder, realtor, or lender; what their biggest challenges were; and what they wish they had known before they started. Learning from others helps you avoid costly mistakes and build realistic expectations.

Once you've gathered insights from your network, the next step is to connect with key professionals who can guide you through the process. Your realtor is your first key professional partner. A Realtor—with a capital R—is a licensed agent and member of the National Association of Realtors. This membership holds them to a higher ethical standard and ensures they have access to ongoing training and professional resources. A great Realtor will understand your goals and budget, help you evaluate properties or lots, provide insight into market conditions and trends, and assist with zoning, permitting, and builder selection. Avoid agents who rely solely on confidence without experience, and be cautious of "deal killers" who focus more on what can go wrong than on how to make it work. Choose someone who listens closely, communicates clearly, and brings substantial building experience to the table.

In a perfect world, you wouldn't need an expert—but in reality, choosing the wrong person can carry real risks. The right Realtor can make all the difference, so choose wisely.

It is also important to know who your realtor represents.

A buyer's agent works for you, advocating for your interests in the transaction. A seller's agent represents the seller, meaning their loyalty lies elsewhere.

Some agents try to act as dual agents. While this is legal in many places, it can create conflicts of interest. In most cases, you are better served with an agent who represents you exclusively.

And always ask about how they are paid. With the new changes in Realtor compensation, it is very important to address this immediately with your representative. Typically, their commission comes from the seller or the transaction, not directly from you. Still, it is important to understand the arrangement.

Next, connect with a lender who understands construction financing. This is very different from traditional home loans.

A construction loan funds the building process in stages, while a mortgage is what you secure once the home is complete. Many lenders offer a construction-to-permanent loan, which simplifies the process. Your lender should help you understand what you can afford, walk you through all fees, closing costs, and timelines, communicate with your builder during each stage, and offer flexible and fair loan terms. Always get multiple quotes—compare rates, closing fees, and overall service. Ask questions and take notes. This is your money and your future..

Once your financing is in place, you will need to identify a title company. A title company plays a central role in the closing process. They conduct the title search, handle escrow funds, and ensure the legal transfer of ownership. You can choose your own title company, even if the builder or lender suggests one. However, a skilled Realtor typically maintains an established relationship with a reputable title company. This connection can offer you additional leverage, as the title company has more at stake—delivering poor service could jeopardize a long-standing partnership with your Realtor. Their commitment to maintaining that relationship often translates into a higher standard of service for you.

The same guidance may hold true with the mortgage company choice. Make sure to ask about all fees in advance, compare a few companies before choosing, and avoid companies that add unnecessary administrative or processing fees. The title company protects your investment, and a trusted provider will make closing smooth and secure.

With the closing process underway, it's important to remember that a successful homebuilding journey begins long before the foundation is poured.

It starts with thoughtful planning and strategic decisions. Begin by shaping your dream through practical steps, answering the Big Three questions: how much you can afford, where you want to build, and what fits your needs. Build your professional team starting with a trusted Realtor and lender, and use your network to gather recommendations and real-world advice. Educate yourself on the roles of title companies, loan structures, and local conditions.

Now, let's take the next step and lay the financial groundwork for building your dream home.

CHAPTER 2

AN IN-DEPTH LOOK INTO HOW MUCH HOUSE YOU CAN AFFORD

BEFORE GROUND IS EVER broken or a single nail is driven, the first and most defining step in the homebuilding journey is financial clarity. Dreaming of the perfect home is natural, and it's an exciting stage filled with possibilities. But if a solid, well-informed financial plan does not support those dreams, they can quickly turn into stress, regret, or costly missteps.

Many homeowners start the building process with only a vague sense of affordability, often tied to what a lender says they *qualify* for. But what you're approved for and what you can *truly afford* are often two very different things.

Determining Actual Affordability

Affordability is more than a number on a pre-approval letter. True affordability is the intersection of three key elements: financial qualification (what your lender will allow), personal comfort (what you can pay without losing sleep), and lifestyle goals (what you can afford without sacrificing your broader financial future).

Let's break those down.

Financial Qualification

Lenders assess your income, debt load, credit score, and assets to determine what loan amount they're willing to offer you. They use financial ratios (covered in detail later) to evaluate your borrowing potential.

But lender qualification is the ceiling, not the target.

Personal Comfort

What is your emotional tolerance for debt? Knowing that 30% of your income goes toward housing, can you maintain peace of mind? What if your partner changes jobs or you decide to return to school? Comfort is subjective, but essential.

Lifestyle Goals

Affordability must account for future planned vacations, kids' college funds, business investments, and early retirement. A mortgage payment that limits your ability to pursue other goals may be affordable in technical terms, but unaffordable in the broader context of your life.

Life is not static. Financial planning for homeownership must include thoughtful preparation for the unexpected.

Every homeowner is subject to risks—job changes, health issues, economic downturns, inflation, or shifts in family needs. Good planning does not eliminate risk, but it reduces the impact of unforeseen events.

A smart strategy includes maintaining an emergency fund—aim for three to six months of living expenses set aside in liquid savings before building; choosing flexible loan terms—avoid over-committing to short loan durations if they strain monthly cash flow; scenario planning—consider "what if" situations like one income being lost or needing to relocate sooner than planned; and avoiding budget overreach—stay well within your means to protect against future financial strain.

Being proactive today can prevent hard choices tomorrow.

One of the best ways to avoid financial stress is to take a conservative, long-term approach to home investment.

Many successful homeowners take a conservative approach to spending and borrowing. They choose homes priced well below their maximum loan qualification, use fifteen-year mortgages not to take on higher payments but to reduce interest costs, make extra payments when financially comfortable while retaining flexibility, and delay luxury features in order to build equity and financial stability first.

You can still build a beautiful, functional home without straining your finances. Often, restraint during construction allows for greater opportunities later, whether that's an upgrade, investment property, or early retirement.

By making mindful choices during the homebuying and building process, you set yourself up for long-term financial health. But smart financial planning doesn't stop there—it extends into how you structure your mortgage itself.

Understanding Discount Points

Taking a conservative approach also means looking for ways to reduce long-term costs, especially when it comes to your mortgage. Many buyers consider purchasing discount points to lower their interest rate.

Discount points are fees paid directly to the lender at closing in exchange for a lower interest rate. One point typically equals 1% of the total loan amount. For example, on a $500,000 loan, one discount point would cost $5,000.

This practice is often referred to as "buying down the rate." The benefit is a lower monthly mortgage payment and, over time, less total interest paid.

How Discount Points Work

One point usually lowers your rate by 0.25%, though the exact amount may vary depending on market conditions. As a general rule, the more points you buy, the lower your rate. However, there is a point of diminishing returns. For this reason, they are most beneficial when you plan to stay in the home for a long time.

It's worth noting that buying discount points has advantages and disadvantages. On the plus side, they can lead to lower monthly payments and less interest paid over the life of the loan. They also help hedge against rising rates. However, there are downsides to consider. The upfront costs are higher, and the break-even point may be several years down the line. In some cases, it may even be better to invest the money elsewhere, depending on your overall financial strategy.

Whether it makes sense to use discount points depends on several key factors. One important consideration is how long you plan to stay in the home. If you expect to stay for ten or more years, the long-term savings may justify the upfront cost. However, if you plan to move or refinance within five years, you may not break even.

Your available cash at closing is another factor to weigh. Because points add to your closing costs, it's important to evaluate whether you have enough funds. If you're tight on cash, it may be wiser to prioritize building reserves and covering moving costs first.

Interest rate trends also influence the decision. If rates are high but expected to drop, paying for points may not be the best move. Conversely, if rates are stable or climbing, buying points can provide predictable savings over time.

To bring this to life, consider the story of Chloe and Charlie Brier, a young couple in their early thirties with two children and a strong desire to build a home. Both are professionals and work closely with their Realtor, Gracie, who connects them with Zoey, a seasoned mortgage consultant.

After reviewing their income, credit, and assets, Zoey informs them that they qualify for a home up to $1,000,000. While they're thrilled, they're also hesitant. Both Zoey and Gracie encourage them to think beyond what they qualify for and instead consider what they can afford while still saving, living comfortably, and planning for the future.

As they review their budget, goals, and preferred neighborhoods, they ultimately decide on a home priced at $825,000—well below their maximum. This decision leaves room for several important financial choices. They're able to purchase discount points to lower their rate, build a generous emergency fund, and keep their monthly payments manageable without compromising their lifestyle.

In the end, Chloe and Charlie's approach reflects intentional, informed planning. By choosing sustainability over excess, they felt confident moving forward with their home purchase.

Understanding how they arrived at that decision requires a look at some of the fundamental tools lenders use to assess borrowing ability. Two key financial ratios play a major role in determining how much a buyer can realistically afford: the "front-end and "back-end ratios." The front-end ratio represents the percentage of your gross monthly income that goes specifically toward housing expenses. A common benchmark is 28%. For example, if you earn $10,000 per month, your housing costs—including mortgage, taxes, and insurance—should ideally not exceed $2,800.

The back-end ratio takes a broader view. It includes all your monthly debt obligations, such as housing costs, credit cards, auto loans, and student loans. Most lenders prefer this number to stay under 36–43%, depending on the type of loan. So, if your total monthly debt payments go beyond $4,300 on a $10,000 income, you may be above the threshold considered acceptable. Still, these figures are guidelines, not hard rules—and your own comfort level might be well below those limits.

Just as Chloe and Charlie evaluated their full financial picture, it's important to consider how your home choice aligns with your lifestyle and long-term goals. Buying or building a home should never come at the cost of financial freedom. Ask yourself whether you'll still be able to travel, save for college, or contribute meaningfully to retirement. Consider whether your budget depends on future raises just to afford today's payments, or if you're giving up too much flexibility in exchange for more space.

Ultimately, the best home supports—not dictates—your lifestyle. Take time to evaluate your current expenses and look ahead. Think about how your needs might change in the next five to ten years. Smart planning now lays the foundation for a richer, more balanced life in the future.

Recommendations for Financial Planning in Homebuilding

Here are specific steps you can take to ensure financial readiness:

1. **Start with a detailed household budget.** Understand where your money is going now and how a new mortgage will change things.

2. **Get pre-approved—not just pre-qualified.** Pre-approval involves documentation and a deeper financial review.

3. **Use financial calculators and modeling tools.** Evaluate scenarios with different down payments, interest rates, and loan terms.

4. **Consult a financial advisor.** Get an outside perspective that includes retirement planning, tax impacts, and broader wealth management.

5. **Review your plan every quarter.** As you progress through the build, revisit your budget and goals to adjust where needed.

6. **Plan for long-term ownership.** Consider resale value, neighborhood growth, and how the home will serve you over time.

Determining how much house you can afford is one of the most powerful steps in the homebuilding journey. It sets the tone for the entire process and helps ensure that the home you build brings joy, not stress.

Building your dream home is a milestone, but only when it fits within a sustainable, intentional financial framework. This is not about building the biggest home. It is about building the *right* home that reflects your values and supports your life for years to come.

CHAPTER 3

IDENTIFYING WHERE YOU CAN BUILD BASED ON YOUR BUDGET

ONCE YOU'VE ESTABLISHED a clear understanding of your financial comfort zone, the next major step in the homebuilding process is determining *where* you can build—and *what* you can reasonably build within that area.

This phase is where your vision begins to take form in practical ways. It's the point where dreams meet design, where preferences must be prioritized, and where the realities of land costs, neighborhood options, and home features start to influence each other in meaningful ways.

It can be both exciting and sobering. You may discover opportunities you never considered, or you may find that some of your original expectations need to be adjusted. Either way, this is a defining stage of your homebuilding journey.

Let's explore the tools, strategies, and insights that will help you identify the right location and the right features based on your budget.

Determining Priorities

Before you begin searching for neighborhoods or viewing floor plans, you need to clarify your *priorities*. These are the non-negotiables that will guide every decision that follows.

Ask yourself if being in a top-rated school district is essential. Consider whether you need four bedrooms for your family to function comfortably, or if a two-car garage, a home office, or a backyard pool is part of your must-haves.

Be honest about what you truly need versus what you simply want.

Once you've clarified those priorities, it's equally important to recognize the role of trade-offs in the process. Every budget, no matter how large, involves compromises. The goal isn't to get everything—it's to get the right things. For example, if a top school district is your highest priority, you may need to adjust expectations around square footage or luxury finishes to stay within budget. Similarly, if four bedrooms and a two-car garage are must-haves, you might need to explore neighborhoods slightly farther from your ideal location. Being flexible on the things that matter less will help you secure the things that matter most.

Let me add: if you're going through this process with a significant other, it's especially important to communicate openly, express concerns thoughtfully, and approach decisions with kindness and a spirit of compromise. This journey will inevitably teach you a bit more about each other. My mother used to say, "If I can carry a little water so you're not overburdened, I should always do that… happily." Negotiate in good faith, celebrate the compromises with a high five, and remember that two perspectives almost always lead to a stronger outcome. The finished product will be a reflection of your shared vision and cooperation, and what could be better than that?

Exploring Floor Plans

After understanding your priorities and making necessary trade-offs, the next step is exploring available floor plans that align with your budget and preferences. The floor plan is essentially the blueprint of your lifestyle. It shapes how you move through your home each day, how you host guests, how your family grows, and how efficiently your home functions.

To evaluate floor plans effectively, start by walking through model homes in the neighborhoods you're considering. This gives you a tangible sense of space and layout that photos or renderings simply can't provide. Additionally, use online tools like Trulia, Realtor.com, or builder websites to compare floor plans side by side. Be sure to look for base pricing as well, making sure the plan itself fits within your budget before you begin customizing features or adding upgrades.

As you explore floor plans, it's important to remember that flexibility is key. Most builders offer some level of customization with their plans. For example, you might be able to add or remove walls, convert a dining room into a study, or extend a garage and adjust room sizes. However, these changes often impact the overall cost, so it's essential to keep communication open with your builder as you explore your options.

Creating a Priority List

As you consider flexibility and customization with your builder, it's helpful to create a clear priority list to guide your decisions. This involves brainstorming all the features you'd love in your new home and then sorting and ranking them based on importance and budget constraints.

For example, your initial draft list might include a top-rated school district, a swimming pool, a two-story family room, four bedrooms, hardwood floors, a two-car garage, attic storage, and a home office. While this list is a great starting point, it's important to recognize that not everything may fit within your budget.

By reorganizing your list to distinguish between essential needs and desirable extras, you can prepare to make smart compromises if necessary. A budget-conscious reordered list might prioritize the school district, four bedrooms, two-car garage, home office, hardwood floors, and attic storage, with the swimming pool and two-story family room listed as nice-to-haves rather than must-haves. This approach helps ensure you focus on what truly matters while keeping your financial goals on track.

When faced with competing priorities, it's often wise to prioritize the features that would be most difficult—or even impossible—to add later. For example, incorporating a first-floor study during initial construction is far more practical than attempting to add one down the road. In contrast, amenities like a pool can typically be added later. Thinking strategically in this way can help you make more informed and future-proof decisions.

Choosing a Neighborhood and Lot

After setting your priorities, your next step is identifying the right neighborhood and available lots because where you build is just as important as what you build. When considering neighborhoods, consider commute times and how far you're willing to travel to work or school.

Also, consider community amenities such as parks, trails, or shopping centers that may be important to your lifestyle. Be sure to understand any homeowner association (HOA) restrictions or fees that may apply. Additionally, pay attention to growth trends to determine if the neighborhood is appreciating.

After all, a great floor plan in the wrong neighborhood is rarely a satisfying long-term choice.

When it comes to lot considerations, several factors come into play. Topography is important—flat lots are easier and cheaper to build on, whereas sloped lots may increase foundation costs or require retaining walls. Often, sloped lots take away from pool or play areas in the backyard.

Orientation also matters; south-facing lots may receive better natural light, while corner lots can offer more privacy but require more maintenance. Easements and setbacks are legal limitations that affect how and where your home can be placed. Finally, elevation can influence the views you enjoy, with higher lots potentially offering better scenery and increasing site preparation and overall cost.

With these general lot characteristics in mind, it's crucial to dive deeper into important considerations that can reveal hidden value or lead to unexpected cost increases. Paying close attention to these details can save you time and money during the building process.

Topography remains a key factor; while a flat lot usually means lower costs and easier construction, sloping lots may look dramatic but often require additional grading, drainage, and foundation work.

Lot size and shape also matter; a large lot in a desirable area might seem like a bargain, but it's essential to assess how much of that space is actually usable and how well it aligns with your floor plan. Irregularly shaped lots, for example, may limit driveway placement or backyard space.

Building restrictions are another critical aspect to consider. **Entitlements** refer to the legal approvals needed to build on a lot, while **setbacks** define how far your home must be positioned from the property line. **Easements** grant utilities or neighbors legal access across certain parts of your property, and **encroachments** occur when structures cross legal boundaries, potentially creating long-term legal issues.

Another important consideration is the condition of neighboring lots. Take time to observe the surrounding properties. Look across the street for things like a cluster of RVs in a driveway, or check whether a rear neighbor's elevated patio compromises your backyard privacy. I recommend physically standing in the front, back, and side yards to take in the full context of the setting. Make sure you're comfortable with the views and the overall feel of the surroundings—you'll be living with them every day. Feel free to knock on the neighbor's door, introduce yourself, and ask questions. You never know what you may learn, and these "free" conversations could save you trouble and expense. Understanding all of these factors will help you make a more informed and confident lot selection.

Site Conditions

After thoroughly evaluating lot selection and legal considerations, it's essential to assess the site conditions before committing to a lot.

Having your builder or a trusted third-party inspector evaluate the site can uncover potential challenges early.

This assessment includes soil testing to determine if the ground is stable enough to support a foundation, as poor soil may require expensive reinforcement. Drainage is another critical factor; standing water or inadequate drainage can increase long-term risks.

Natural obstructions like trees, boulders, or buried debris can also raise preparation costs. At the same time, man-made conditions— such as the placement of streetlights, fire hydrants, driveways, electric transformers, and sidewalks—should be considered as they affect your home's layout and access. If you have concerns about any of these issues, consider making your offer contingent upon a satisfactory review of those items. Including such contingencies provides you with the opportunity to address potential red flags before fully committing to the purchase.

In addition to site conditions, it's important to understand the difference between a plat and a survey. A **plat** is a general map of the development showing lot boundaries and the community layout. In contrast, a **survey** is a detailed legal document that specifies your particular lot's dimensions, boundaries, and any easements or encroachments. Reviewing both carefully before finalizing your purchase helps avoid surprises and legal issues down the road.

Remember: if you are not perfectly clear on the words or phrases of the trade, Google and ChatGPT are always a quick cheat sheet.

Financial Considerations

When it comes to financial considerations, be wary of the trap that "cheap is not free." In land and homebuilding, a deeply discounted lot may come with costly site preparation requirements, zoning challenges, or other limitations that prevent you from building the home you want. Think long-term: Is the lot inexpensive because it's undesirable or unbuildable? Will it cost more to prepare or maintain? And will it hold or increase in value over time?

I am reminded of Zig Ziglar's recommendation when it comes to price. He said:

> *"Why settle for the 'good buy' when in the long run the good costs less? It is unwise to pay too little. When you pay too much, you lose a little money—that is all. When you pay too little, you sometimes lose everything because the thing you bought was incapable of doing what it was bought to do. The common law of business balance prohibits paying a little and getting a lot."*

I think this is great advice.

On the other hand, strategic spending can pay off significantly. For example, choosing a better school district may boost future resale value. Paying more up front for a lot with simpler grading could save you thousands in site preparation costs. Similarly, opting for a slightly smaller home in a better location may provide greater appreciation over time. Trust your budget, but be willing to spend smart when it comes to long-term value.

As you move forward, managing your budget alongside your priorities becomes a critical balancing act where planning meets discipline. While exploring floor plans, lots, and features, it's important to regularly evaluate what is most important to you, what fits within your budget, and where you might be willing to compromise. Keeping these questions in mind helps maintain focus and prevents overspending or regret later in the process.

At this stage, flexibility is your greatest asset. The earlier you make decisions grounded in realistic priorities, the less likely you are to face difficult, pressured choices down the line. Waiting until construction has begun to cut features often leads to rushed and emotional decisions. It's far better to make the tough calls upfront—before the pressure mounts—so you can move forward confidently and with clarity.

Recommendations

Here are practical tips to guide you through this decision-making phase:

1. **Create a master list of wants and needs.** Prioritize based on long-term importance.

2. **Research multiple neighborhoods and communities.** Compare cost, location, and growth potential.

3. **Walk lots in person.** Pictures rarely tell the full story.

4. **Work with professionals.** Your builder, Realtor, and lender should all help you make decisions about lots and floor plans.

5. **Build in a buffer.** Allow for unexpected costs related to land, permits, or site prep.

6. **Document everything.** Keep a journal on each lot or plan your visit. Decisions blur over time.

7. **Be realistic.** A perfect home is rare. A smart, well-balanced home is more achievable and more satisfying.

8. **Be grateful.** There will be bumps; temper them on balance with your blessings.

Identifying where you can build based on your budget is a thoughtful, layered process. It requires clarity about your finances, honesty about your priorities, and discipline in your decision-making.

The better your planning now, the smoother the road ahead will be. By balancing dreams with data, and emotion with strategy, you are well on your way to building a home that's not only beautiful, but smart, sustainable, and tailored to your life.

CHAPTER 4

CONTRACTING WITH
THE BUILDER

SO FAR, YOU'VE clarified your budget, identified your priorities, and explored floor plans and neighborhoods. Now, you arrive at one of the most pivotal stages of the homebuilding journey: selecting your builder and entering into a legally binding construction contract.

This chapter is where everything begins to formalize. Your choices become commitments. Your expectations must be documented. Your budget becomes real, enforceable, and testable.

Contracting with a builder is not a formality—it is a cornerstone. It shapes the nature of your relationship with your builder, the clarity of communication throughout the build, and the financial outcome of your investment.

This chapter will guide you through how to evaluate different builder types, contract structures, pricing models, negotiation points, financing considerations, and common pitfalls. This is where diligence, patience, and professionalism matter most.

Understanding Builder Types and Their Limitations

Many people assume that once they have a lot and a floor plan, they can hire any builder and proceed. The reality is far more nuanced.

Builders are highly specialized. Each builder operates within a business model tailored to a specific type of customer, construction method, budget range, and level of customization.

The Four Main Builder Categories:

1. Custom Builders

Custom builders offer maximum flexibility in design, materials, and layout. They often build on your land or help you locate a suitable lot. These builders typically involve higher costs and longer timelines, requiring more buyer involvement and decision-making. They are common for high-end or architect-designed homes.

2. On-Your-Lot Builders

On-your-lot builders are either semi-custom or production builders who construct homes on lots that the buyer already owns or chooses separately. They allow more flexibility than tract builders but less than fully custom builders. Usually, they offer a portfolio of plans with modifiable options.

3. Production/Tract Builders

Production or tract builders build the same set of plans repeatedly within planned communities. They offer limited customization, usually upgrades within a pre-set catalog. These builders provide economies of scale and faster build times. The builder typically owns and develops the lots, making this category common for suburban developments or master-planned communities.

4. General Contractors

General contractors are independent operators who coordinate construction. They are often used for major renovations or truly one-off builds and require the buyer to handle more preconstruction work, such as plans, permits, and materials. In my experience, general contractors are less likely to offer optimal service, expertise, or professionalism to first-time clients. I would approach the situation with caution.

The type of builder you choose will significantly impact your experience throughout the homebuilding process. Your chosen builder type affects how much customization you will have, what level of design support is included, how pricing and contracts are structured, and how much of the process you must manage yourself.

Before committing to a builder, being honest about your preferences is important.

Customization: Balancing Vision with Reality

The allure of customization is strong—many buyers begin with a romantic vision of designing their home exactly how they want it. This impulse is completely natural since building a home is a rare opportunity to create a space perfectly tailored to your family's needs. However, the deeper you dive into full customization, the more complexity, delays, and expenses you may encounter. That's why experienced builders often encourage finding a balance between personalization and practicality.

One of the key advantages of working with production or on-your-lot builders is the value of repetition. Plans that have been built multiple times tend to be priced more accurately, built more quickly, and are less likely to face structural or permitting issues.

Additionally, these homes are often easier to resell because their functionality has been proven over time. Most production and on-your-lot builders offer a portfolio of pre-engineered plans that provide cost-effective starting points. If a plan meets 80–90% of your needs, it's usually wiser to modify it slightly rather than design entirely from scratch.

Pricing

Pricing a custom home in the abstract is like asking, "How much does a sack of groceries cost?"

The answer: it depends. It depends on obvious factors such as market conditions, design complexity, and level of personalization. Still, let's bring some clarity to the conversation. Below is a rough, rule-of-thumb breakdown of estimated costs by category:

1. Lot / Land Acquisition: 15%–30%

This varies significantly by location.

- In urban or coastal areas, the lot can represent 30% or more of the total budget.
- In rural or suburban areas, it may fall closer to 15%–20%.

2. Hard Costs (House Construction): 50%–60%

This includes materials, labor, framing, foundation, roofing, mechanical systems (HVAC, plumbing, electrical), and finishes.

- Custom homes using premium materials or complex designs can push this percentage higher.

3. Soft Costs: 10%–25%

This includes:

- **Design & Professional Fees** (architect, engineer, interior designer): 5%–15%
- **Permits & Impact Fees**: 1%–5%
- **Financing Costs** (interest, loan fees, etc.): 1%–5%
- **Insurance** (builder's risk, liability): 1%–3%
- **Surveys, Soils Reports, Utility Tap Fees**, etc.

Understanding Contracting Methods

After selecting the right builder and understanding the type of customization and building approach that meets your needs, the next crucial step is to focus on how you will formalize your agreement. Understanding contracting methods is an important part of this phase because the contract you enter into will clearly define what will be built, how it will be built, who pays for what, how conflicts are resolved, and what happens if circumstances change along the way. This is also where you will need the assistance of a talented realtor, lawyer, and/or mortgage representative to review the documents.

There are two primary contractual structures to be aware of. **The first involves separate agreements for the lot and the house.** In this approach, you have one agreement with the seller of the lot, who may be the builder, a developer, or a private owner, and a separate construction agreement with the builder. This method offers flexibility in choosing your builder, sourcing your lot, and managing financing. However, it also means you own the land before construction begins, increasing your upfront responsibility. Additionally, you will need to manage two separate closings, which can bring extra costs and coordination challenges.

The second structure is a combined purchase agreement common among production builders. Here, a single agreement covers both the lot and the house, simplifying financing and closing processes. These contracts often include incentives for using the builder's preferred lenders or title companies. The trade-off is a limited ability to negotiate or select your own vendors, and you must generally use the builder's plans and process. But let's be honest, you are most likely ill-suited to recommend contractors, and most builders would not permit it anyway.

Regardless of the structure, it's critical to understand key contract clauses. These include deposit requirements and refund conditions, allowable timeline changes due to factors like weather or materials, specifications for change orders and upgrades, how disputes will be resolved—whether through mediation, arbitration, or litigation— and warranty terms, along with how post-close repairs are handled. Knowing these details upfront helps protect your investment and ensures smoother progress throughout the build.

Choosing the Right Floor Plan

Once you've navigated the contracting process and have a clear agreement with your builder, choosing the right floor plan is the next important step, especially for custom builds. It's not enough to simply love a plan on paper; the design must be compatible with your chosen lot.

This means considering factors such as the size, shape, and orientation of the lot, as well as setbacks, easements, and grading requirements. Additionally, neighborhood zoning rules and HOA design guidelines may impose further restrictions.

Your builder should provide a detailed lot fit analysis to ensure a proper fit. This analysis overlays your selected floor plan onto the exact survey, showing critical measurements, setbacks, driveway access, and utility lines to confirm everything aligns.

Another essential consideration involves entitlements and restrictions, which refer to the legal permissions required to build your home. These include zoning approvals, design reviews in HOA communities, septic permits or water tap availability, and any regulations related to tree removal or environmental setbacks. While your builder typically handles these aspects, you remain responsible for confirming that the home you plan to build is both legally permitted and practically feasible on your lot. A well-chosen title company will provide a representative who will review your survey and the title of the property in detail with you. It is their job.

Making Selections

After confirming that your chosen floor plan fits your lot and complies with all legal and practical requirements, you'll move into the design selection phase—arguably the most exciting and potentially most expensive part of the homebuilding journey.

Once your plan is finalized, you'll begin making selections for your home's appearance and features. On the exterior, you'll choose elements like brick, siding, stone, paint, roof color, windows, and doors. Inside, you'll select flooring, cabinets, countertops, plumbing fixtures, lighting, and paint colors. You'll also decide on optional features such as fireplaces, built-ins, decks, or extra rooms that enhance both functionality and style.

At this stage, it's also important to consider site-related factors. For instance, if you plan to add a pool later, avoid installing irrigation in that area. Be sure to coordinate sewer, electric, and gas lines to prevent costly rerouting in the future. Confirm underground utility routes before finalizing any exterior design features that might interfere. Ask your builder for a detailed selection schedule so you know when each decision must be made in order to stay on the timeline.

Understanding Pricing

As you dive into selections, understanding how pricing works will help keep your budget in check.

The base price advertised by a builder typically includes the basic floor plan, standard finishes, the builder's standard lot if applicable, and some allowance for landscaping or appliances. Many buyers also look at price per square foot, which is a misleading metric. It varies significantly depending on house size (smaller homes often cost more per square foot), design complexity (rooflines, elevation changes, and unique angles add cost), and lot preparation (sloped or wooded lots are more expensive to build on). Use price per square foot only as a rough estimate, not a precise budgeting tool.

Builders also use different pricing models; understanding these is key to financial planning.

In a **cost-plus model**, you pay the actual cost of materials and labor, plus a fixed fee or percentage for the builder. This model offers full transparency but can lead to fluctuating final costs—best suited for custom homes and high-trust relationships. Acknowledging the significant effort involved in reviewing construction invoices is also important.

Without a clear understanding of industry norms—such as waste factors, material overages, or breakage and theft—there is a risk of misinterpreting standard practices as mismanagement or negligence. This misunderstanding can erode trust between the buyer and builder and ultimately diminish the overall enjoyment of the homebuilding experience.

The **fixed price with true-up model** offers a fixed base price, but allows adjustments if material costs rise beyond a set threshold (i.e., 5–10%), balancing predictability with real-world flexibility. This is often used in volatile markets.

A **traditional fixed price model**, on the other hand, provides one final number agreed upon at contract signing. Unless you change the scope or selections, the price won't change. This model is ideal for buyers seeking financial certainty and minimal oversight. Keep in mind that the builder may round up certain contingency items, as they will not have the opportunity to charge for them later. This is likely a *de minimis* amount and one that would typically be absorbed within other pricing models.

Remember, though, that there's more to your budget than construction costs alone. A comprehensive budget includes both hard and soft costs. Hard costs cover land acquisition and site development, such as clearing, grading, utilities, materials, labor, subcontractors, permits, and inspections. Soft costs include loan interest during construction, property taxes, insurance, utility connection fees, HOA dues, and legal or closing costs. Building a spreadsheet or using budgeting software can help you track all these categories accurately.

Of course, even with careful planning, common budget busters can derail your financial goals. These often include upgrading finishes after the contract, particularly flooring and cabinets, unexpected site issues such as poor soil or buried debris, custom structural changes late in the process, underestimated soft costs like interest and insurance, and rushed decisions made under pressure. To protect yourself, it's wise to build a 5–10% contingency into your total budget from the start. This cushion allows for flexibility and peace of mind as your dream home begins to take shape.

Writing and Executing the Contract

Once your selections are made and your budget is finalized, you'll move into writing and executing the contract. This agreement sets the foundation for how your home will be built and under what terms, so it's essential to approach it with care and attention.

Several parties are typically involved in this stage, including the builder's sales representative, your Realtor if one is assisting you, your lender, and the title company. Each plays a role in reviewing, drafting, or facilitating parts of the agreement, but ultimately, you are the one signing off, so you need to be fully informed.

Make it a priority to review every page of the contract carefully. Don't hesitate to ask questions about any clauses you don't understand. Consider consulting an attorney to review the terms if your builder uses a custom contract. Custom contracts can contain provisions that favor the builder, so it's important to understand exactly what you're agreeing to.

In contrast, state-approved contracts tend to be more neutral and standardized, offering a more balanced framework. Regardless of which type is used, ensure that you clearly understand your rights, obligations, and any potential risks. This is your opportunity to clarify expectations and protect your investment before construction begins.

Choosing Your Financing

With your contract in place, the next step is choosing your financing, and it's best to begin discussing loan options as early as possible. By this point in the process, you should already have a clear understanding of your financial position. That said, let's explore a few important nuances.

One common route is a **construction-to-permanent loan**, which converts into a standard mortgage once your home is complete. Payments on this type of loan are typically made in **draws** as different phases of the construction are finished, helping to fund the build in stages.

How a Construction-to-Perm Loan Works

1. Loan Application & Approval (Before Construction Starts):

- You apply with a lender, who evaluates your credit, income, builder qualifications, plans, specs, and land value.
- The lender approves both the **construction phase** and the **long-term mortgage** simultaneously.

- You typically lock in the **permanent mortgage interest rate** upfront.

2. Construction Phase (Draw Period):

- The loan funds are disbursed in stages called **draws** as construction milestones (e.g., foundation, framing, drywall) are completed.
- You typically make **interest-only payments** on the amount drawn during this phase.
- The lender may send an inspector before releasing each draw.

3. Conversion to Permanent Mortgage (After Completion):

- Once the home is complete and a **certificate of occupancy** is issued:
  - The loan automatically converts to a permanent mortgage **of your choice** (usually a 15–30 year fixed or adjustable-rate loan).
  - You begin making regular principal + interest payments.
- No need to requalify or pay closing costs again—**one closing covers both phases.**

Pros:

- One set of closing costs (vs. two if you did separate construction and mortgage loans).

- Rate lock protection if rates rise during construction.
- Simplifies paperwork and the financing process.

Cons:

- Requires a qualified builder and approved plans/specs.
- Usually, credit/income standards are higher than those of a regular mortgage.
- May require a larger down payment (typically 10–20%).

Another option may be **builder-offered financing**. Builders often provide incentives such as paid closing costs or interest rate buy-downs if you use their preferred lender. While these offers can be appealing, it's important to compare them against third-party lenders. What may seem like a great deal on the surface could cost more in the long run, so be sure to look at the full picture.

As you explore loan options, focus on the total monthly cost, which includes principal, interest, taxes, and insurance. Also consider escrows, construction interest, closing fees, and any required reserves. To make an informed decision, ask each lender for a Truth-in-Lending document.

Truth in Lending refers to a federal law, the **Truth in Lending Act (TILA),** which was enacted in 1968 to promote informed use of consumer credit by requiring clear disclosure of key loan terms and costs.

Key Points:

- **Purpose:** To protect consumers from deceptive lending practices and ensure lending terms transparency.
- **What It Requires Lenders to Disclose:**
  - **Annual Percentage Rate (APR):** The total cost of borrowing, expressed as a yearly rate.
  - **Finance Charges:** The total dollar amount the loan will cost, including interest and fees.
  - **Payment Schedule:** Number, amount, and timing of payments.
  - **Total of Payments:** Sum of all payments over the life of the loan.
  - **Total Amount Financed:** How much you're actually borrowing (not including interest or fees).

Closing on the Property

Once your financing is in place, you'll prepare to close on the property. This typically happens at the title company, where final documents are signed and funds are transferred. At closing, you'll be responsible for the earnest money deposit, any option deposits for upgrades and selections, loan costs, prepaid taxes and insurance, and applicable survey or inspection fees.

Be sure to request an **ALTA Settlement Statement** (formerly known as a HUD-1) for a detailed breakdown of all costs. Confirm your title insurance coverage and ask for a clear explanation of how prorated taxes and insurance are calculated. Most importantly, double-check all wiring instructions with your title company directly—wire fraud is a serious risk, and extra caution at this stage is essential to protect your funds.

Recommendations for a Smooth Contracting Process

1. **Interview multiple builders.** Do not choose based on price alone.

2. **Document everything.** Confirm all selections, upgrades, and changes in writing.

3. **Review contract timelines.** Understand deadlines, penalties, and grace periods.

4. **Avoid emotional decisions.** Sleep on large upgrades or changes before approving.

5. **Track costs weekly.** Build and maintain a simple spreadsheet.

6. **Communicate professionally.** Treat your builder like a business partner, not a vendor.

7. **Don't rush the contract.** Take your time to read, ask, and understand.

8. **Remember.** If you do not have it in writing, you likely are not getting it. Not for any nefarious reason, but in these negotiations, things change, memories fade, and the possibility of genuine misunderstanding is always present. Get it in writing!

Contracting with a builder is where planning turns into action. It's the single most significant agreement of the homebuilding process—setting the tone for budget, communication, quality, and timelines.

The more informed you are, the better your experience will be. Clear contracts, honest budgets, and professional communication are what separate smooth builds from stressful ones.

CHAPTER 5

THE BUILDING PROCESS —UNDER CONSTRUCTION

AFTER MONTHS OF BUDGETING, planning, meetings, and paperwork, the most thrilling part of the homebuilding journey finally begins: construction. This is when vision becomes structure, when ideas take form, and when your new home starts rising from the ground.

While the legal and administrative steps that precede construction—such as financing and contract execution—are vital, they can feel abstract and procedural. Now, you enter a phase that is tactile, visual, and deeply personal.

This chapter is your guide to the construction phase: how it works, what you need to do, and how to stay involved. We'll explore selections, customization, builder coordination, and the common pitfalls to avoid. Most importantly, you'll learn how to enjoy this part of the process—because it should be fun, engaging, and immensely satisfying.

The Fun and Excitement of Making Selections

One of the most interactive parts of construction is the **selections process**—choosing the finishes and features that will define the look, feel, and function of your home. From cabinets to countertops, flooring to faucets, these decisions bring your personal style to life.

As you learned earlier, selections typically occur around the same time you're completing the contract and loan paperwork. This can be an overwhelming period, as you're managing deadlines, making financial decisions, and facing multiple choices about your home's design. Staying organized during this time is essential.

Selections are usually divided into stages, often following a builder's internal timeline:

1. **Exterior selections**
2. **Kitchen and bath design**
3. **Flooring and lighting**
4. **Final design sign-off**

Working through these stages systematically will keep your build on schedule and your decisions aligned with your budget.

Exterior Selections: Setting the First Impression

Curb appeal matters. Your home's exterior is the first thing you'll see each day, and the first impression guests will have. It's also one of the few permanent, unchangeable aspects of your home, so it deserves careful consideration.

Exterior options may include a wide range of materials and finishes. You'll choose between brick, stone, stucco, or various siding styles. Paint or finish colors for trim, shutters, and doors, roofing materials and colors, garage doors, porch columns, and exterior lighting fixtures are also part of the process.

To make confident choices, keep a few key principles in mind.

- **Aim to balance boldness with timelessness.** While it can be tempting to choose trendy finishes, exterior colors are difficult and expensive to change once installed.

- **Visiting model homes is incredibly helpful.** Seeing materials in person provides a much clearer sense of texture, scale, and color than digital samples or swatches.

- Finally, be sure to **check your neighborhood's guidelines**; some communities limit exterior color palettes or require design approval for certain finishes. Taking the time to get this right will pay off every time you pull into your driveway.

Interior Selections: Making It Yours

Interior selections have the biggest impact on how your home feels every day. These are the details that shape your experience—how your kitchen functions, how your bathroom feels, and how your home reflects your personality and lifestyle.

Once again, I encourage you to visit model homes in your area. While some may hesitate to do this, it's a common practice, and onsite sales representatives are very accustomed to it. In fact, many are happy to offer guidance, and discussing selections and design choices is often their favorite part of the job.

The Kitchen

The kitchen is the heart of the home, and here, you'll make several critical decisions. Cabinet choices include style, finish, and hardware, all of which set the tone for the space. Countertop materials may range from quartz and granite to solid surface or laminate, depending on your budget and aesthetic. The backsplash gives you a chance to add texture and personality, with a wide range of tile patterns, materials, and grout colors to choose from. Appliances are another major consideration, including the finish, layout, and special features like built-in ovens or range hood vents. These choices affect not just how your kitchen looks, but how well it supports your daily routine.

The Primary Bathroom

In the primary bathroom, you'll select vanities based on layout, sink configuration, and cabinetry finish. Tile plays a starring role in the shower, floor, and accent areas. Fixtures like faucets, lighting, and towel bars tie everything together. You'll also choose between soaking tubs, rain showers, or more standard bath-shower combinations.

Your selections in the kitchen and bathrooms should strike a balance between beauty and function. Think about how you live—how you cook, how you relax—and design accordingly.

Flooring and Lighting: Function Meets Atmosphere

Flooring and lighting selections also shape the atmosphere of your home.

For flooring, you might choose hardwood for its durability and timeless appeal, though it comes at a higher price. Luxury vinyl plank offers a stylish and water-resistant alternative that's more budget-friendly. Tile works well in kitchens and bathrooms, while carpet remains an affordable choice for bedrooms and secondary living areas.

Lighting design deserves just as much attention.

Overhead fixtures like recessed lights, chandeliers, or flush mounts define the general tone of a room. Task lighting, including under-cabinet lights or pendant lights above islands, improves function in specific areas. Accent lighting—such as decorative sconces or statement fixtures—adds personality and visual interest. The right lighting elevates everything, from mood to practicality.

Additional Features and Special Touches

Finally, consider any additional features and finishing touches that could enhance daily life. Fireplaces, whether gas or wood-burning, offer both comfort and style, with options to customize the surrounding materials. Built-ins like bookshelves, entertainment centers, or mudroom benches create efficient use of space and add character. Outdoor living upgrades—such as covered patios, decks, or pergolas—extend your usable space and add value. And don't forget landscaping, which might include initial plantings, irrigation systems, and sod installation.

Many of these features are easier and more cost-effective to include during construction rather than retrofitting later.

While it's tempting to customize everything, every change has a cost, both financial and timeline-related. Builders have systems and workflows built around their standard designs. Deviating too far can create delays, confusion, and errors.

Discuss all customizations early and get written approval. Also, ask: "Will this change affect my completion date?" "Will this change require permit modification?" "What is the cost of this change?"

To approach customization in a balanced way, focus on structural changes during planning. Make design upgrades within the builder's standard options where possible. If you plan future upgrades (like a pool or outdoor kitchen), tell your builder so infrastructure (electric, gas, and drainage) can be prepped now.

Extra Space

In my view, living space is one of the most important considerations when purchasing a home. Cosmetic features—such as upgrading from carpet to hardwood flooring, or even adding a swimming pool—can often be addressed later, sometimes with just a modest investment or tax return. However, living space is typically a permanent element of the home.

Most builders offer options like family room extensions or bay windows in the breakfast area, which can significantly enhance your daily living experience. Take the time to thoughtfully consider where you and your family will spend the most time and whether the space supports comfort, enjoyment, and functionality.

In the case of space, and I don't say this often, but in this instance, I believe it is better to spend a little more than you planned rather than less than you should. Above all, ensure the layout and size of your new home are a fit for your lifestyle, now and in the future.

Coordination with the Builder

As construction gets underway, clear communication becomes essential. Stay in sync on selection deadlines, as builders often have strict timelines. Understand change order policies—know the cutoff dates and fees for mid-build changes. Walkthroughs and site visits are also important. Regular check-ins help catch issues early.

Throughout the process, work with the designated point of contact—usually a project manager, superintendent, or sales representative. Be respectful of the builder's processes while advocating for your needs. Remember, building a home is collaborative. Builders appreciate clients who are proactive, communicative, and clear.

However, no matter how carefully you plan and coordinate, building a home can, I will say, will present unexpected challenges. It's important to anticipate these issues so you can navigate them with less stress.

For example, delays are common and can result from weather conditions, inspections, supply chain disruptions, labor shortages, and sometimes builder errors. You might also encounter mismatched materials, such as tiles or paint batches that vary slightly from what you expected. Budget creep is another frequent challenge, as small upgrades and changes can quickly add up. Additionally, decision fatigue can set in when faced with too many options over time, making it harder to stay focused.

To effectively manage these challenges, keep detailed records by tracking every change, selection, and timeline adjustment. Creating a digital or physical binder with plans, invoices, and correspondence helps maintain organization and clarity. It's also wise to expect minor delays and build some flexibility into your move-in schedule. Finally, confirming all decisions in writing prevents misunderstandings and keeps everyone on the same page throughout the process.

Remember, building a home involves millions of parts, thousands of documents, and hundreds of people—most of whom are working outdoors. With so many moving pieces, challenges are not only possible, they're predictable. Experienced builders understand this, which is why it's important to trust the process. When an issue arises, approach it with a "let's solve this" mindset rather than "how could this happen." Every challenge has a solution, and it will be resolved. Then life—and your new home—will move forward.

Finalizing Selections

Generally, your selections must be finalized before framing begins. This step is essential because it ensures that materials can be ordered, inspections scheduled, and trade partners coordinated without delay.

Checklist Before Final Approval:

1. **Review every selection for accuracy.** (Seriously, do this!)
2. **Confirm appliance dimensions match cabinetry.**
3. **Verify structural changes on architectural drawings.**
4. **Ask about any back-ordered items or substitutions.**
5. **Get a signed confirmation of your selections from the builder.**

This is your last chance to make changes without triggering fees or delays.

To help navigate this stage smoothly, stay organized by using spreadsheets or selection books to track your decisions. Bringing samples home can be invaluable since colors and finishes often look different under natural versus artificial light. Focus your upgrades on key areas like kitchens, bathrooms, and primary living spaces, which tend to offer the best return on investment. Ask plenty of questions and clarify timelines, specifications, and options—never assume anything.

Finally, keep all communication professional and concise. Builders manage many clients simultaneously, so clear emails or checklists will help you stand out.

The construction phase is where your home begins to take shape, physically and emotionally. From choosing finishes to managing timelines, this is a dynamic time of decision-making and anticipation.

The best homes are built on a foundation of thoughtful decisions and collaborative effort. As construction continues, you'll soon find yourself standing in the rooms you once imagined on paper.

In the next chapter, we'll take you to the finish line: walkthroughs, inspections, final payments, and preparing for moving day.

It's time to bring your vision fully to life.

CHAPTER 6

CROSSING THE FINISH LINE

THE END IS IN SIGHT. After months of planning, selecting, constructing, and coordinating, you're approaching one of the most anticipated moments in your homebuilding journey: completion.

This final phase of construction brings a mix of emotions—excitement, relief, impatience, and sometimes even anxiety. Your dream home is nearly finished, but it also demands patience, clear communication, and thoughtful action.

It's easy to feel overwhelmed during these last few weeks. The site is buzzing with trades, touch-ups are happening everywhere, and you may start noticing small imperfections or unfinished details. That's all part of the process.

In this chapter, we'll walk you through what to expect during the final stages of construction, how to prepare for your final walkthrough, how to manage the punch list, and how to plan your move with confidence. We'll also discuss the often-overlooked transition from *construction project* to *homeownership*.

Let's guide you across the finish line—with purpose, preparation, and pride.

Final Stages of Construction

What's Happening On-Site

During this stage, painters begin applying both interior and exterior finishes, while electricians install light fixtures and switches throughout the home. Plumbers are busy fitting faucets and testing water systems to ensure everything functions properly. Flooring and tile are laid or finalized, adding texture and warmth to each space. Cabinets, doors, and hardware are installed, giving shape to kitchens, bathrooms, and storage areas. Appliances arrive and are connected, and critical systems like HVAC units, water heaters, and ventilation systems are activated to prepare the home for occupancy.

It's a high-energy environment with multiple trade partners on-site, often working simultaneously. While the excitement builds, it's important to recognize that restrictions on on-site visits may increase during this phase for safety, efficiency, and liability reasons.

Trust your builder's process. Frequent updates, photos, and guided visits will keep you informed without interfering with the final push toward completion.

Managing Concerns and Expectations

During this phase, it's natural to shift from excitement to scrutiny. As your home nears completion, you may begin to notice small imperfections—flaws that hadn't caught your eye before. Scratches, uneven paint lines, missing hardware, or leftover debris can suddenly make your dream home feel a bit less than perfect.

This is normal. Every new home, no matter how well-built, will have minor cosmetic or finish issues that need correction at the end. Don't panic—this isn't a sign of poor construction. It's simply part of the process when dozens of trade partners are converging to complete work on a tight timeline. Document your concerns and keep a running list of what you see. These items will be addressed, most during the **punch list process**. It's important to relax and know that your builder expects this stage and is prepared to address it.

Handling the Last-Minute Details

As those early imperfections are noted and documented, the final stretch of construction shifts into addressing last-minute details. This phase involves hundreds of small but critical finishing touches that bring the home to its final form. Repainting touch-up areas, adjusting doors and drawers for proper alignment, caulking tile and trim, cleaning construction debris, testing water pressure and temperature, and programming thermostats and smart home systems all take place during this time.

Your builder will coordinate these tasks with subcontractors, vendors, and inspectors to ensure everything is fully functional, safe, and visually complete, delivered with both care and precision.

At this point, communication becomes more important than ever. It's a time for clear, professional, and proactive engagement with your builder's project manager, superintendent, or sales representative. Ask for a final schedule so you're aware of key installations, inspections, and walkthroughs. Document any concerns using email or a shared document to keep a running list. Be available for timely approvals or clarifications if your builder reaches out. And above all, respect the process—builders are under significant pressure at this stage, so being firm yet fair helps everything move forward smoothly. A good builder will appreciate your engagement, especially when it's respectful, organized, and focused on solutions.

The Final Walkthrough

Once the final details have been addressed and communication with your builder is flowing smoothly, the process moves toward one of the most important milestones: **the final walkthrough**. This is your opportunity to inspect the finished product and ensure that everything is complete or will be completed according to the agreement.

Come prepared with a copy of your contract and design selections, your documented list of concerns, a phone or notepad for additional notes, and a clear, focused mindset.

During the walkthrough, pay close attention to paint quality and wall surfaces, cabinet alignment, and hardware functionality. Make sure all doors and windows open and seal properly. Check that plumbing fixtures work without leaks, flooring is free of damage or visible defects, appliances are installed and functioning, and all electrical outlets and switches operate as expected. Test everything— open doors, run faucets, turn on lights.

It's important to ensure the home meets the standard you've planned and paid for.

The Punch List

After the final walkthrough, you'll collaborate with your builder to create a **punch list**, or a detailed record of items that need to be corrected, repaired, or completed either before closing or shortly afterward. This step ensures nothing is overlooked and gives both parties a clear plan for resolution.

Common punch list items include:

- Paint touch-ups
- Scratched fixtures or floors
- Misaligned cabinet doors

- Missing or incorrect hardware
- Window or door adjustments
- Minor trim or tile fixes
- Appliance issues

The builder will review and confirm the list, communicate timelines for completing each item, and may schedule a follow-up visit before closing. Most builders will also address smaller items after closing through their warranty process.

Remember that while this process may feel unique and unfamiliar to you, your builder has been through it countless times. Many of the items you've identified are intentionally scheduled to be completed during the final phase of construction—commonly referred to as the **punch-out stage**. In most cases, these items are not missed or overlooked; they are simply part of the planned final touches. Builders often catch and complete details that even homeowners may not have noticed.

Throughout this stage, it's important to be fair and realistic. Focus on legitimate concerns rather than striving for absolute perfection. Builders want to deliver a complete and polished product, and most take pride in making sure it meets your expectations.

Preparing for Homeownership

Once your punch list is finalized and the key systems in your home are operational, it's time to start preparing for move-in day. But this moment deserves patience, not haste. Plan your move carefully by considering the timing of completed punch list items, final inspections, and utility setup, as well as the receipt of your certificate of occupancy, which provides legal permission to inhabit the home.

To ensure a smooth transition, hire movers who offer some flexibility in case of unexpected delays. Label your boxes by room to make the unpacking process easier, and aim to schedule large deliveries, such as furniture and decor, for a few days after your move-in. This helps reduce clutter and allows space to get settled. Take time to deep clean the home—or better yet, hire a professional cleaning service—before you start unpacking. Moving into a new home is a major life event, and treating it with preparation and grace can make all the difference.

Final Inspections and Approvals

Before you can legally move into your new home, your builder and local building authorities will need to conduct a series of final inspections. These may include evaluations of your electrical, plumbing, and mechanical systems, checks for proper grading and drainage, and inspections to ensure smoke detectors and CO_2 monitors are up to code. Your home must also meet all applicable energy code requirements. Once everything passes, you'll receive a **certificate of occupancy**. Be sure that all required approvals, certificates, and warranties are obtained and documented before your closing.

Before You Move In

Leading up to move-in, there are a number of important tasks to handle to ensure your transition is seamless. Set up your utility services, including electric, gas, water, internet, and waste collection. Don't forget to install blinds or window treatments—these are often not included with your build. Schedule mail forwarding and update your address with banks, employers, healthcare providers, and other important contacts. Be sure to finalize your home insurance and confirm that the coverage aligns with your lender's requirements.

We offer a few final recommendations to help you stay grounded during this phase.

Stay organized by using digital tools or a physical binder to keep track of everything, from punch list items to utility account information, warranties, manuals, and all communications with your builder.

Be proactive in anticipating possible delays and maintaining backup plans. Being a step ahead with documentation and scheduling will save you stress. And finally, stay positive. The final stretch of the homebuilding process can be frustrating, but it's also incredibly rewarding. Don't let small imperfections steal your joy. This is the home you've envisioned, planned, and built from the ground up.

Crossing the finish line is about more than construction. It's about transitioning from a project to a home, from blueprints to memories.

Every detail, every delay, and every decision has brought you to this point. Now, the real journey begins—not as a builder or buyer, but as a homeowner.

In the next chapter, we'll explore what comes after the keys are handed over and how to thrive in long-term homeownership and protect the investment you've worked so hard to build.

Let's continue the journey, now, as proud owners of your dream home.

CHAPTER 7

MOVING DAY AND LIVING IN YOUR DREAM HOME

THE LONG-AWAITED MOMENT has arrived. The final nail has been hammered, the last fixture installed, and the paint has dried. It is time to move into your dream home. This moment is often accompanied by a mix of emotions—excitement, exhaustion, relief, and even a little anxiety. After all the planning, decisions, and construction phases, it is easy to think the hard work is over. But while the construction journey may be ending, the journey of homeownership is just beginning.

Moving day is not simply a logistical event; it is a rite of passage. It is the moment your house becomes your home. And like all transitions, it requires preparation, awareness, and care. This chapter is designed to guide you through the final steps before and after you move in, from dealing with permits and utilities to understanding structural warranties, creating maintenance schedules, and managing common post-move challenges.

Living in your dream home should be joyful, but it is also a responsibility. With the right mindset and preparation, you will be able to settle in with confidence, knowing how to protect and care for the home you've worked so hard to build.

Final Preparations Before Moving In

Before you start unpacking boxes and arranging furniture, a few critical steps must be completed to ensure your move is legal, safe, and well-organized.

Use and Occupancy (U&O) Permit

The process starts with obtaining a **Use and Occupancy (U&O) permit**. This document, issued by your local municipality, certifies that your home has passed all final inspections and is officially deemed safe for habitation. Without it, you cannot legally move in. While your builder is generally responsible for coordinating with the local inspector and submitting the required documentation, you should request a copy for your own records. Confirming that this permit has been issued is vital before scheduling movers, accepting deliveries, or setting up your utilities. The U&O also serves as confirmation that major systems—like electrical, plumbing, and HVAC—are fully operational and meet all code requirements.

Converting from a Construction Loan to a Mortgage

If you financed your new home with a construction-to-permanent loan, this is also the time to transition into your long-term mortgage. This process involves a final inspection by your lender to verify that the home is complete, followed by a review of all funds that have been disbursed. The lender will then issue a final loan package for your signature and officially establish the terms of your permanent mortgage. These terms will include your finalized interest rate, payment schedule, and any escrow account details. It's important to confirm every detail with your lender, including when your first mortgage payment is due, how that payment should be made, and whether your monthly obligation has changed from earlier estimates.

Setting Up Essential Services

As move-in day approaches, it's critical to make sure all essential services are set up in advance. This will help you avoid disruptions in utilities and reduce stress during your transition. Ideally, you should contact your electric, gas, and water providers about two weeks before your scheduled move to ensure services are active on your arrival date. Schedule installation for internet, cable, or satellite TV, and inform your waste management provider of your new address and start date.

You'll also want to submit a change-of-address form with the U.S. Postal Service and update your driver's license and vehicle registration if required by your local jurisdiction.

Additional services such as home security, lawn care, or pest control are also worth setting up as you begin to settle into regular home maintenance.

Understanding Your Structural Warranty

Another critical step during this phase is understanding your structural warranty. One of the major advantages of building a new home is having the peace of mind that comes from this type of coverage, but not all warranties are created equal. A **structural warranty** generally covers key components that are essential to the home's safety and integrity. This typically includes load-bearing walls and beams, foundation systems, roof framing systems, joists and trusses, and floor systems. The coverage period for these elements is usually six to ten years, though it may vary depending on your builder and the specific warranty provider.

Warranty Types and Timeframes

1. **One-Year Workmanship Warranty:** Covers cosmetic and surface-level issues such as drywall cracks, nail pops, paint touch-ups, and minor trim issues.

2. **Two-Year Systems Warranty:** Covers electrical, HVAC, and plumbing systems that fail due to workmanship or installation errors.

3. **Structural Warranty:** Covers major load-bearing elements that affect the safety or livability of the home. **Structural warranties range from six to ten years.**

Once you understand the general scope of your structural warranty, it's equally important to get clarity on the details of how it is administered and maintained.

Always ask your builder who is responsible for administering the warranty, whether it is handled directly by the builder or through a third-party warranty company.

You should also inquire about the specific claims process. Ask what documentation is required, how long the typical resolution takes, and who to contact when issues arise. Additionally, be sure to confirm whether there are any maintenance obligations you must fulfill in order to keep the warranty valid. Some warranties require regular upkeep or documentation of service, especially for major systems like HVAC or roofing.

Carefully review all warranty documents, including any exclusions or fine print. Once reviewed, store them in a safe and easily accessible place. This documentation may be needed years down the line, and having it organized will make future claims or resale processes much smoother.

Seasonal Maintenance Responsibilities

A new home does not stay new forever unless it is properly maintained. Seasonal maintenance is one of the most overlooked aspects of homeownership, but it is absolutely essential to preserve the value and functionality of your home.

In the spring, your focus should be on cleaning and preparing for warmer months. Clean gutters and downspouts to ensure proper drainage, power wash siding and walkways to remove grime, and test your sprinkler systems. It's also a good time to check window caulking and weatherstripping, and to service your air conditioning system to ensure it's ready for summer.

Summer is ideal for inspecting and protecting your home's exterior. Check and reseal outdoor wood surfaces like decks or fences, inspect attic ventilation and insulation, touch up exterior paint and sealant, and clean fans, vents, and range hoods to maintain good indoor air quality.

As fall approaches, it's time to prepare your home for colder weather. Clean your chimney and fireplace, service the furnace and replace filters, winterize irrigation systems and outdoor faucets, and, once again, clear leaves and debris from gutters to prevent blockages.

During winter, pay special attention to areas vulnerable to cold weather. Check for ice dams on the roof and inspect it after storms, monitor your basement for leaks or condensation, keep walkways free of snow and ice to prevent slips, and test your sump pump and any backup power systems.

Creating a checklist or calendar for these tasks ensures you stay consistent year after year. A little time spent each season goes a long way in protecting the value, efficiency, and longevity of your home.

Preventive Maintenance Planning

In addition to seasonal maintenance, developing a preventive maintenance plan is essential for keeping your home in top condition year-round. While seasonal tasks focus on weather-related upkeep, preventive maintenance is about catching wear and tear before it becomes a costly problem. These smaller, recurring tasks can be done monthly or quarterly and are vital for the long-term performance of your home's key systems.

For example, replacing your HVAC filters every one to three months helps your heating and cooling systems run efficiently and maintains indoor air quality. Flushing your water heater annually prevents sediment buildup, which can reduce efficiency and shorten the unit's lifespan. Cleaning dryer vents not only helps your appliance work better, but also significantly reduces the risk of fire.

It's equally important to test your smoke and carbon monoxide detectors regularly to ensure they're functioning correctly. Periodically inspecting your foundation for cracks or signs of settling can alert you early to structural concerns that might otherwise go unnoticed.

Be sure to document each maintenance task, noting the date it was completed, the service provider, if one was used, and any observations or repairs made. Keeping a thorough maintenance log not only helps you stay organized but also provides a strong record for warranty claims or when it's time to sell your home.

Preventive care is one of the smartest investments you can make as a homeowner, saving money, protecting your home's value, and offering peace of mind.

Moving Day Logistics and Challenges

Even after all the planning, preparation, and anticipation, the day you move into your new home can feel like organized chaos. Moving day is a major milestone, but it often comes with a whirlwind of logistics, last-minute decisions, and physical exhaustion. While the excitement is real, so are the risks, especially when it comes to protecting your brand-new finishes, floors, and walls.

Common moving day challenges include accidental damage caused by movers, like scratched trim, dented walls, or scuffed flooring. Large furniture may not fit easily through doorways or staircases, leading to frustration or unexpected delays. And once everything is inside, the sheer volume of boxes and decisions around where things go can quickly lead to overwhelm.

To protect your home—and your sanity—during the move, take a few simple precautions. Lay down floor runners and install corner guards in tight spaces to shield your finishes. Prioritize unpacking essential boxes first, such as those with bedding, toiletries, and kitchen basics. Clearly label each box and aim to unload room by room instead of piling everything in one area. Keep cleaning supplies close at hand so you can quickly manage spills or dirt. And most importantly, take a break during the day to reset and breathe.

If any damage does occur, document it immediately with photos and notify your moving company, as reputable movers should have insurance to cover such incidents.

Common Post-Move Issues

As you begin to settle in, don't be surprised if you start noticing issues that weren't obvious during your final walkthrough. Living in a space often reveals small imperfections or quirks that only emerge with regular use. These are usually minor, but still important to track and communicate to your builder if they fall under the warranty period.

You may discover things like nail pops or small drywall cracks, uneven heating or cooling between rooms, doors or windows that stick slightly due to settling, squeaky floors or stairs, or changes in grout color, or separation in tile lines.

Start a running list and submit it in writing to your builder. Many builders offer formal check-ins at the thirty-day and eleven-month marks specifically to address these post-move items.

Reasonable Expectations for Fixes

It's also important to understand what to expect when it comes to warranty service and repairs. Your home will naturally continue to "settle" throughout the first year as materials adjust to changing humidity and temperatures. Builders anticipate this and are typically prepared to make adjustments.

Most cosmetic concerns will be addressed within a few weeks, while larger system issues—such as HVAC or plumbing—will be prioritized. However, because builders depend on various trade partners for follow-up work, repair timelines may vary.

To help everything go smoothly, continue communicating clearly and respectfully, and keep a written record of requests and responses. Patience and persistence go a long way. Remember, your relationship with your builder doesn't end at closing—it continues throughout your warranty period and sometimes even longer.

After navigating the move-in process and addressing early post-occupancy concerns, your focus will gradually shift from completing the build to truly living in and caring for your new home. This transition marks the beginning of a long-term relationship with your property, and how you approach it will shape your experience for years to come.

To make the most of this new chapter, we offer a few guiding principles.

- **First, stay organized.** Create a dedicated homeownership binder or digital folder where you can store warranty documents, appliance manuals, receipts, utility account information, and a running maintenance log. Having all this information at your fingertips will make it easier to schedule repairs, file warranty claims, or plan future improvements.

- **Second, stay proactive.** Don't wait for things to go wrong. Preventive and seasonal maintenance, like cleaning gutters, servicing HVAC systems, and checking seals or caulking, will extend the life of your home's components and help you avoid costly surprises down the road.

- **Third, stay realistic.** Even in a brand-new home, imperfections will exist. It's important to remember that homes are built by people, not machines. While you should expect a high standard of craftsmanship and accountability, absolute perfection is neither possible nor sustainable. Focus instead on the overall quality and livability of your space.

- **Finally, stay positive.** Building a home is the result of months or even years of planning, decisions, and emotional investment. As you settle in, take time to appreciate what you've created. Celebrate the milestone. Embrace the learning curve. The minor flaws you notice now will soon fade into the background as your new home becomes the backdrop for your life.

Moving into your dream home is a landmark moment. It represents more than just the conclusion of a construction process—it symbolizes the beginning of a new chapter. A home filled with potential, memories yet to be made, and opportunities for growth.

You are not just moving into a new house. You are stepping into a space that reflects your values, your lifestyle, and your future.

As you settle in, your home will evolve. Your style will change, your needs will shift, and your family may grow. Embrace that journey. Plan your future upgrades, from landscaping to smart technology. Take your time to personalize your home at your own pace.

The dream of homeownership is not static—it grows with you. Enjoy it. Nurture it. And take pride in what you have built.

CHAPTER 8

CREATING SYNERGY THROUGH EDUCATION

BEHIND EVERY SUCCESSFUL home build is not just a talented builder or a well-thought-out design, but a cohesive, informed, and aligned team. From the first conversation to the final walkthrough, the quality of communication, understanding, and trust among all parties involved determines whether the experience is smooth or stressful, rewarding or frustrating.

Whether you are a homeowner, real estate agent, contractor, or lender, engaging in open dialogue and continuous learning ensures everyone is rowing in the same direction. When participants are educated and empowered, the results speak for themselves: fewer surprises, greater satisfaction, and a stronger sense of partnership.

The Value of Shared Knowledge

Transparency is the cornerstone of any successful project. In homebuilding, that means honest conversations about how the budget is structured, which selections are locked in versus those still changeable, what timelines are realistic, and how delays might impact progress. It includes site-specific realities such as grading challenges, easements, or municipal building codes, and it also means understanding the ripple effects of design changes made late in the process.

When expectations are vague or information is withheld, even small miscommunications can turn into major frustrations. But when everyone involved shares information openly and early, most challenges can be managed, or even avoided altogether.

This openness extends naturally into the value of education. Homebuilding involves a stream of complex decisions: What type of loan is best? How do you choose between hardwood and engineered wood? Why are certain lots more expensive to develop? These aren't just logistical questions—they're deeply emotional, tied to personal values, daily habits, and long-term dreams. When builders take the time to educate clients, it builds trust. It shows respect for the client's investment, not just financially, but emotionally, and transforms the experience from a transactional one into a true partnership.

And that partnership works best when all participants are fully engaged. For homeowners, this means leaning into the process instead of feeling overwhelmed by it. Education reduces stress and builds confidence. When clients understand why a decision matters or what constraints exist, they're less likely to second-guess and more likely to enjoy the process.

To get there, homeowners should feel encouraged to ask questions early and often, to thoroughly read through contracts and selection documents, to come to design meetings prepared with ideas and notes, and to document any decisions or changes in writing. Visual tools like floor plans, mood boards, and digital galleries can also make complex choices easier to grasp.

When homeowners are active participants rather than passive observers, they become true collaborators, an approach that improves outcomes and makes the entire experience more rewarding for everyone involved.

The Role of Trade Partners and Suppliers

Just as homeowners benefit from clarity and education, so do the professionals who help bring a home to life.

Subcontractors and suppliers play a critical role in the building process, not just for their technical expertise, but as vital links in the communication chain. Educating them on the broader project goals, the client's vision, and specific expectations minimizes misunderstandings and fosters a sense of ownership over the final result.

This means going beyond simply assigning tasks. It involves providing clear scopes of work and realistic timelines, sharing relevant client feedback and desired outcomes, and encouraging trade partners to speak up early if they see potential issues.

Recognizing and respecting their contributions also strengthens the working relationship.

When trade partners feel valued and informed, they're far more likely to deliver quality work with care and commitment.

In this dynamic, the builder plays a central and unifying role, like an orchestra conductor. While the job certainly includes managing budgets and schedules, it also requires something more nuanced: the ability to foster a culture of communication, clarity, and collaboration. Builders who proactively educate clients and coordinate with trade partners help every part of the process flow more smoothly.

They can do this by hosting kickoff meetings that align everyone on project goals, timelines, and roles; providing written guides that help clients understand each phase of construction; responding to questions in writing to maintain clarity and accountability; and using shared platforms or documents to ensure everyone has access to up-to-date information.

When builders take the lead in this way, they reduce confusion, prevent costly errors, and create an environment where each participant feels confident, supported, and motivated to do their best work.

Creating a Collaborative Culture

Creating a collaborative culture in homebuilding starts with recognizing that no single person builds a home alone. Every new home is the product of a network—builders, designers, engineers, trade partners, lenders, city officials, realtors, and, of course, the homeowners themselves. When these participants understand not only their individual responsibilities but also how their roles intersect, the process becomes more cohesive and productive.

Realtors can play a vital role by educating buyers about construction timelines and expectations. Lenders can clarify draw schedules, escrow requirements, and financial checkpoints so there are no surprises. Builders can explain how design decisions affect scheduling and cost. And homeowners can contribute by clearly sharing their lifestyle needs and long-term goals.

When this level of cooperation is achieved, potential conflicts are often replaced with constructive dialogue, and small misunderstandings become opportunities for better alignment.

The Benefits of Educated Clients and Teams

A well-informed project team is easier to work with, and educated participants are more confident in the decision-making process, less likely to be disappointed by realistic compromises, and better prepared for delays or unforeseen issues. They tend to communicate more respectfully and constructively, which reduces stress for everyone involved. Most importantly, they're more likely to refer friends and family or leave positive reviews when the dust settles.

Ultimately, this is how reputations are built. Not just through the quality of the finished product, but through the quality of the experience along the way.

To close, we recommend a few core principles to keep that culture of clarity alive.

- **Start with education.** Begin every relationship with a strong foundation of knowledge. When the entire team understands the big picture, they are better equipped to navigate the details.

- **Repeat key information.** People forget what they hear. Reinforce important topics through multiple touchpoints—in writing, in meetings, and in follow-ups.

- **Encourage questions.** The best clients are the ones who ask. Questions show engagement. Welcome them and answer with clarity and patience.

- **Use multiple learning formats.** Not everyone learns the same way. Use visuals, written guides, conversations, and real-world examples to make information stick and your questions resonate.

- And finally, **make it a team culture.** Everyone on the team, from sales to construction to the buyer, should buy into the value of education. It is a mindset, not a task.

That's how strong homes are built, from the ground up, and from the inside out, with shared understanding leading the way.

CONCLUSION

FROM DREAM TO DOORSTEP—THE JOURNEY OF BUILDING A HOME

YOU'VE MADE IT to the end of this book, but in many ways, this is just the beginning. Whether you are standing on the threshold of your new home or still considering the path ahead, take a moment to reflect on what brought you here: the dream of creating something entirely your own.

This book was written to serve as your trusted guide through the homebuilding process. It was designed to demystify what can feel overwhelming and to offer clarity where there is often confusion. Our goal was to empower you with the knowledge and confidence to navigate one of the most significant investments and personal journeys of your life.

Yes, you're building walls and foundations, kitchens and bathrooms, decks and driveways. But more importantly, you're building the stage for a life well-lived.

A home is the canvas upon which you will raise children, host celebrations, build relationships, and find peace. It is a place for laughter, milestones, quiet mornings, and busy evenings. Every detail you planned—the cabinet pulls, the flooring, the open spaces, the cozy corners—will come to life through daily living.

That is the real reward. Not just the satisfaction of completing a build, but the opportunity to make this space your own and fill it with what matters most.

The Long-Term View

As you transition from builder to homeowner, remember that your responsibility doesn't end at closing. Your home is a living environment that requires ongoing care, attention, and stewardship.

You'll find that maintenance, repair, and eventual improvements are part of the natural rhythm of homeownership. Your floors may scuff, your roof may someday need repair, and your needs may evolve. But your understanding of how your home was built and your commitment to its care will serve you well for decades.

Create habits of care. Schedule seasonal check-ins. Keep warranties and manuals accessible. Stay connected to your builder or service network for ongoing support.

Most importantly, take pride in what you've created.

If you're reading this conclusion at the start of your journey, we invite you to take the first step today. Sit down and articulate your vision. Start making a list of what you want. Begin conversations with your family, a realtor, or a lender. This book has given you the roadmap—now it's time to take the first real step.

If you're already in the process, continue using the tools and insights from this book as a framework. Revisit chapters as you enter new phases. Share the lessons with your partners, your builder, and your team. Let this book be more than a read—make it your reference.

And if you've just finished your build, congratulations. Take a deep breath. Walk slowly through your new home. Soak it in. And then begin to live. Host that dinner. Plant that tree. Hang that photo. Build a life inside the space you once only imagined.

We want this to be the beginning of an ongoing relationship. Our team at Herzog Homes is dedicated to education, service, and long-term value. Whether you're planning your build, in the middle of it, or years into homeownership, we're here to support you.

Click the link or scan the QR code to access:

https://qrkit.co/ZGaFQ1

- Video guides and walkthroughs
- Seasonal maintenance checklists
- Financing calculators
- Design inspiration and updates
- Contact information for scheduling consultations or follow-up services
- Special announcements from Herzog Homes

SCAN ME

Building a home is about creating more than structure. It's about forming a foundation for living, dreaming, and growing.

You are not just a client. You are a creator, a visionary, a homeowner. You took the bold step to build something lasting. We hope this book helped make that process clearer, more confident, and ultimately more rewarding.

On behalf of everyone at Herzog Homes, thank you for allowing us to be part of your journey.

Here's to your home. Here's to your future. Here's to building it well.

Warmest regards,

David Herzog